D0722910

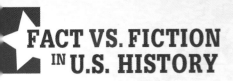

FACT VS. FICTION IN U.S. HISTORY

PAUL
REVERE
AND THE MIDNIGHT RIDE:
SEPARATING FACT FROM FICTION

by Danielle Smith-Llera

CAPSTONE PRESS
a capstone imprint

Capstone Captivate is published by Capstone Press, an imprint of Capstone.
1710 Roe Crest Drive
North Mankato, Minnesota 56003
www.capstonepub.com

Library of Congress Cataloging-in-Publication Data
Names: Smith-Llera, Danielle, 1971- author.
Title: Paul Revere and the midnight ride : separating fact from fiction / by Danielle Smith-Llera.
Description: North Mankato, Minnesota : Capstone Press, [2021] | Series: Fact vs. fiction in U.S. history | Includes bibliographical references and index. | Audience: Ages 8–11 | Audience: Grades 4–6 | Summary: "Many know Paul Revere by the infamous words, "The British are coming!" But did he really say that? Primary sources and infographics help readers learn the facts and the fiction behind Paul Revere's midnight ride"— Provided by publisher.
Identifiers: LCCN 2020044594 (print) | LCCN 2020044595 (ebook) | ISBN 9781496695659 (hardcover) | ISBN 9781496696755 (paperback) | ISBN 9781977154729 (pdf) | ISBN 9781977156389 (kindle edition)
Subjects: LCSH: Revere, Paul, 1735-1818--Juvenile literature. | Massachusetts—History—Revolution, 1775–1783—Juvenile literature. | Statesmen—Massachusetts—Biography—Juvenile literature. | Massachusetts—Biography—Juvenile literature.
Classification: LCC F69.R43 S645 2021 (print) | LCC F69.R43 (ebook) | DDC 973.3/311092 [B]—dc23
LC record available at https://lccn.loc.gov/2020044594
LC ebook record available at https://lccn.loc.gov/

Image Credits
Alamy: Lebrecht Music & Arts, cover (bottom right), 11, Pictorial Press Ltd, 25, Pictures Now, 4; DVIC: NARA, cover (top), back cover, 21; Getty Images: Portland Press Herald/Jack Milton, 17, VCG/Corbis/Barney Burstein, 20, VCG/Corbis/Geoffrey Clements, 24; iStockphoto: traveler1116, 13; Library of Congress: 12, 15; Line of Battle Enterprise: 6; National Park Service: Minute Man National Historical Park, 27; The New York Public Library: 5, 8 (right), 10, 14; North Wind Picture Archives: 18, 19, 22; Shutterstock: Everett Collection, cover (left), 7, 8 (left), 28, m_sovinskii, 23; Wikimedia: Biruitorul, 9

Editorial Credits
Editor: Gena Chester; Designer: Kyle Grenz; Media Researcher: Svetlana Zhurkin; Production Specialist: Katy LaVigne

Source Notes
p. 9, "do not print my name," Letter from Paul Revere to Jeremy Belknap, circa 1798, Massachusetts Historical Society, masshist.org/database/99
p. 11, "Noise! . . ." Elias Phinney. *History of the Battle of Lexington: On the Morning of the 19th April, 1775.* Boston: Phelps and Farnham, 1825, p. 16.
p.12, "glorious band of patriots," Edward Everett. A*n Oration Delivered at Concord, April the Nineteenth, 1825, Volume 16, Issue 1.* Boston: Cummings, Hilliard and Company, 1825, p. 50
p. 15, "a new Revolution," quoted in Jill Lepore's "Paul Revere's Ride Against Slavery," *New York Times,* nytimes.com/2010/12/19/opinion/19Lepore.html
p.23, "We frequently took turns. . ." "Intelligence Throughout History: Paul Revere's Midnight Ride," Nd. Central Intelligence Agency, cia.gov/news-information/featured-story-archive/2010-featured-story-archive/intelligence-history-paul-revere.html
p. 26, "If you go an. . ." Revere's deposition, corrected copy, 1775, The Paul Revere House, www.paulreverehouse.org/the-real-story/paul-revere-capture-site/
All websites accessed on May 28, 2020.

Table of Contents

Introduction 4

Chapter One
Close to the Action................................6

Chapter Two
A Big Anniversary 10

Chapter Three
The Legend 14

Chapter Four
A Team of Patriots 18

Chapter Five
A Risky Journey................................24

Breaking Down Longfellow's Poem.............29
Glossary..30
Read More 31
Internet Sites...31
Index 32

Words in **bold** are in the glossary.

Introduction

Paul Revere floated quietly on a rowboat through the darkness. It was the night of April 18, 1775. Revere was on a risky mission. If British soldiers discovered him leaving Boston at this late hour, they would arrest him. They knew that many American **colonists**, like Revere, were frustrated with British rule. Colonists in the nearby town of Concord, Massachusetts, were even storing weapons!

Paul Revere leaving Boston on a rowboat

In Boston, British soldiers were preparing to march to Concord to take its weapons. Revere heard they would also stop in Lexington to capture **patriot** leaders. He was on his way to sound the alarm.

Revere landed at the nearby town of Charlestown and borrowed a horse. It was close to midnight as he galloped off. According to the popular story, Revere knocked on farmhouse doors and shouted to wake sleeping colonists. Because of Revere, the colonists were ready to defend themselves from the incoming British!

But is that what really happened on his ride?

Chapter One

Close to the Action

In 1775, Revere was considered a loyal patriot—but not a hero. The American Revolution had just begun. It started in Lexington, Massachusetts, on April 19, the morning after Revere started his midnight ride. Armed colonists were waiting at the town center when British soldiers arrived. After a short battle, British soldiers marched to Concord.

The Battle of Lexington

On April 22, patriot leaders in Massachusetts asked hundreds of **eyewitnesses** to write down what they saw. They wanted to prove British soldiers started the violence in Lexington. Paul Revere wrote an **account** of his mission. He scratched out and added details. Then he neatly wrote a final three-page version.

But Revere's account of his ride was not remarkable at the time. That's because he couldn't see much of the battle in Lexington. A house blocked his view.

REVERE'S JOBS

Paul Revere worked as a silversmith and an engraver. He made prints and illustrations for books, magazines, and other businesses. His most famous print shows British soldiers shooting colonists during the Boston Massacre of 1770. Many colonists bought the print. They were already frustrated with Great Britain's unfair laws. Revere's print made them even angrier.

Revere made this print of the Boston Massacre in 1770.

Hunting for Facts

In 1798, historian Jeremy Belknap asked Revere for a new account of his midnight ride. More than 20 years had passed, and Revere was in his 60s. Yet Belknap trusted Revere's memory to uncover more details. Revere also believed his story was incomplete. He wrote an eight-page account in a letter to Belknap.

Several documents help prove that Revere's accounts are accurate. His 1775 account and his letter to Belknap are all stored at the Massachusetts Historical Society. Both of his accounts are similar. Other peoples' accounts of that night are similar to Revere's as well.

Paul Revere

Jeremy Belknap

Belknap published Revere's account in 1798. However, history books in the late 1700s didn't include Revere's name or details about his mission that helped spark a revolution.

Massachusetts Historical Society headquarters in Boston

Fact!

Revere wanted to remain anonymous when Belknap published his 1798 account. Revere wrote "do not print my name" near his signature. His name was published anyway.

Chapter Two

A Big Anniversary

Revere's account of his midnight ride suddenly gained some public attention in 1825. It was the 50th anniversary of the Battle of Lexington. Ten survivors published new accounts in Elias Phinney's book, *History of the Battle of Lexington*. Historians have wondered if they are accurate. They are different from 1775 accounts in at least one major way. They state that Lexington **militiamen** fired the first shot—not British soldiers.

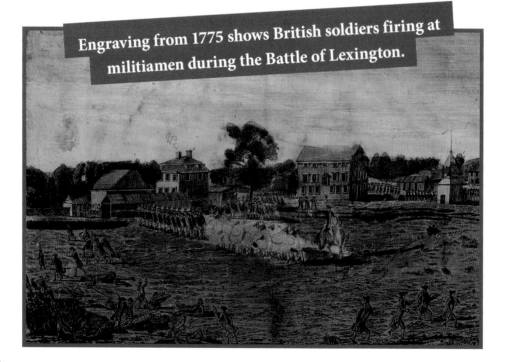

Engraving from 1775 shows British soldiers firing at militiamen during the Battle of Lexington.

In one of these accounts, William Munro remembered guarding the house where patriot leaders were sleeping. When Revere rode up, Munro asked him to make less noise. "Noise!" said Revere. "You'll soon have a noise that will disturb you all. The British troops are on their march, and will soon be among you." Revere's name and a version of his story now appeared in a history book.

Paul Revere warns the guards at the house where Samuel Adams and John Hancock stayed.

Telling the Story

At Concord's 50th anniversary celebration, Edward Everett told an audience the first detailed version of Revere's midnight ride. Everett was a famous public speaker. He spoke about the "glorious band of patriots" who participated in that night's events.

Edward Everett

1882 engraving that shows Paul Revere's ride

Everett based his version of the story on research. Like a historian, he was interested in facts. He studied both Revere's and Munro's eyewitness accounts. Everett's speech was published, which meant it reached a larger audience. In the 1830s, Revere's ride began to appear in new history magazines and books about the American Revolution.

Chapter Three

The Legend

Eighty-five years after Revere's ride, a famous poet named Henry Wadsworth Longfellow toured Boston's Old North Church. In his diary, Longfellow wrote about climbing stairs to the **belfry**. He imagined lanterns hanging there on the night of Revere's ride. The next day, Longfellow started work on a poem about Revere's ride. But the U.S. was on the brink of a new war, which also took up the poet's thoughts—the Civil War.

Henry Wadsworth Longfellow

U.S. states had taken sides over slavery. Longfellow was an **abolitionist**. He felt the nation needed "a new Revolution" to bring enslaved people freedom. Longfellow's poem described Revere as an American hero who started a revolution in 1775. The story was a perfect symbol for the revolution Longfellow hoped for in 1860.

"Paul Revere's Ride" was first published in a popular magazine on sale in December 1860. The first battle of the Civil War took place just a few months later. With the poem's publication, fiction mixed with facts. Revere's ride turned from history into legend.

The U.S. Civil War started with the Battle of Fort Sumter on April 12, 1861.

Fiction and Facts

"Paul Revere's Ride" has entertained readers for more than 160 years. The poem begins like a story: "Listen, my children, and you shall hear/ Of the midnight ride of Paul Revere." Its galloping rhythm and rhyme make the lines easy to memorize.

Longfellow was a professor who knew how to research. There is **evidence** that shows Longfellow probably knew the facts of Revere's story. A biography of Paul Revere was published in a 1832 magazine. Historians believe Longfellow might have read it because he owned a copy of it. Still, Longfellow's poem does not match the facts. Instead, he takes poetic license.

Many poets and authors value the message over exact facts. Poetic license can make a story more interesting and fun. But it can be a problem when people think the fiction in a story is true. In "Paul Revere's Ride," many people did just that.

LISTEN, my children, and you shall hear
Of the midnight ride of Paul Revere,
On the eighteenth of April, in Seventy-five;
Hardly a man is now alive
Who remembers that famous day and year.

He said to his friend, "If the British march
By land or sea from the town to-night,
Hang a lantern aloft in the belfry arch
Of the North Church tower as a signal light, —
One, if by land, and two, if by sea;
And I on the opposite shore will be,
Ready to ride and spread the alarm
Through every Middlesex village and farm,
For the country folk to be up and to arm."

Then he said, "Good night!" and with
        muffled oar
Silently rowed to the Charlestown shore,
Just as the moon rose over the bay,
Where swinging wide at her moorings lay
The Somerset, British man-of-war;
A phantom ship, with each mast and spar
Across the moon like a prison bar,
And a huge black hulk, that was magnified
By its own reflection in the tide.

Meanwhile, his friend, through alley and street,
Wanders and watches with eager ears,
Till in the silence around him he hears
The muster of men at the barrack door,

"Paul Revere's Ride" by Henry Wadsworth Longfellow

Chapter Four

A Team of Patriots

In his poem, Longfellow writes wonderful action, but most of it is inaccurate. He writes of Revere looking back across the river at Boston's Old North Church. Longfellow creates suspense as Revere watches for a message from patriot spies in the city. Revere's horse waits impatiently too. Revere suddenly sees two lanterns shining from the belfry.

Illustration shows Revere seeing the lantern signal behind him, which tells him the British were crossing the river. But Revere's 1798 account proves this isn't what actually happened.

The two lights signaled that the British were crossing the river toward Lexington and Concord. One lantern would have signaled that the British were marching along a different route.

But Revere's 1798 account explains that the lantern signal was not for him. It sent a warning to people across the river, in case British soldiers arrested a messenger like Revere. In fact, Revere had asked two men in Charlestown to light the lanterns—before he left Boston!

Fact!

Matches weren't invented until 1826. This made lighting lanterns in Revere's time tricky. Instead of matches, a bar of steel rubbed against a flint stone created a spark.

The lantern signal in the Old North Church's belfry

Midnight Riders

Revere was the only messenger in Longfellow's poem. The poet describes Revere as a lone hero who carried "the fate of a nation." But it took many messengers to warn so many colonists. In his original 1775 account, Revere explained how it happened.

Patriot leader Joseph Warren sent both Revere and William Dawes on the midnight ride. Dawes was a leather worker and patriot. Both men knew the countryside outside of Boston well. Dawes often traveled there for business. Revere was already an experienced messenger. He carried news and important documents all over New England.

William Dawes

Dawes took a different path from Revere. But they met up in Lexington. From there, they sent more riders to spread the warning. About 40 riders carried the message through the countryside that night.

Illustrations often show Revere making his trip alone, but in reality, many people rode out to warn colonists.

Fact!

In 1878, Henry Ware Holland, a **descendant** of Dawes, published a book called *William Dawes and His Ride with Paul Revere*. Longfellow read it.

A Big Job

Longfellow wrote that Revere's "voice in the darkness" and "knock at the door" woke colonists up. But in real life, Revere did more than simply knock on every door he passed. His work was more complex.

Revere explained in his accounts that he warned town leaders. These leaders then spread the news through their towns. Eyewitness accounts described colonists waking up to a mix of church bells ringing, guns firing, and drums beating.

A militiaman preparing for the Battle of Lexington

Militiamen had been preparing for this moment. They were volunteers who trained like soldiers to protect their towns at a moment's notice. Revere woke the captains of the militiamen. When the British reached Concord, hundreds of militiamen were waiting.

PATRIOT SPIES

Revere was part of the first patriot spy organization. Skilled workers and **artisans**, like Revere and Dawes, were members. They held meetings in Boston's Green Dragon Tavern for 10 years before the American Revolution. They planned raids on British military equipment. They also collected information secretly. Revere wrote: "We frequently took turns, two and two, to watch the (British) soldiers by patrolling the streets all night."

Green Dragon Tavern

Chapter Five

A Risky Journey

Revere's journey to Lexington was not easy and pleasant, as Longfellow describes. In the poem, Revere travels along a peaceful river to the sound of steady hoofbeats. But Revere's accounts show that he faced danger all along the way.

Historians have accounts that describe Revere's journey to Lexington. British General Thomas Gage wrote orders to send British soldiers to watch the road to Lexington. Revere's accounts describe what happened when he crossed paths with two of them.

The soldiers spotted Revere leaving Charlestown and chased him on horseback. Revere was grateful for his horse. He quickly changed his path to escape them. Revere mentioned that one British soldier fell into a pond during the chase!

Fact!

The name of Revere's horse was Brown Beauty. John Larkin, a Charlestown patriot, gave Revere the horse and named it for him.

Paul Revere escaping British soldiers

Mission Accomplished

In Longfellow's poem, Revere completes his mission to Concord. But actually, Revere was captured before he could. Accounts by eyewitnesses and Revere himself prove it.

After midnight, Revere and Dawes rode out of Lexington toward Concord. A third rider, named Samuel Prescott, joined them. Prescott was a patriot and doctor from Concord.

Revere's account explains how a British patrol stopped the trio. It was around one o'clock in the morning, and the messengers were halfway to their destination. Revere recorded the soldiers' fierce words: "If you go an Inch further, you are a dead Man."

Revere's fellow riders escaped. Dawes went back to Lexington. Prescott jumped his horse over a low wall into the woods. Prescott rode to Concord. He was the only one of the three able to finish the mission. The soldiers released Revere but took his horse. Revere returned to Lexington on foot before dawn.

The site of Paul Revere's capture

The True Story

Longfellow's poem has inspired people to know more about Revere. A historian wrote the first long biography about Revere's life in 1891. People have been curious about Revere's artwork too. His elegant works in silver are shown in museums today.

The legend of Revere's ride has made people want to learn more about the night before the American Revolution broke out. People have debated which of Boston's many church steeples held the lanterns.

"Paul Revere's Ride" by Longfellow is considered historical fiction. It captures the general facts of

Paul Revere

Revere's midnight ride. But it expands on those facts. It expresses the patriotism of people taking great risks for their nation.

Breaking Down Longfellow's Poem

Fiction Revere rode alone.

Fact William Dawes headed out of Boston too, but in a different direction. Once they arrived in Lexington, the two messengers organized others to ride into the countryside to help spread the warning.

Fiction Revere needed to see the lanterns in Old North Church to know which way the British were leaving Boston.

Fact Revere knew before he left Boston how the British were traveling to Lexington. Soldiers were taking the shorter path by sailing across the water to Lexington on a warship.

Fiction Revere's ride to Lexington went according to plan.

Fact Revere had to change his route leaving Charlestown because British patrols tried to capture him.

Fiction Revere arrived in Concord to warn the residents the British were on their way.

Fact Revere was stopped by British soldiers on the road outside Lexington. Another rider, Samuel Prescott, galloped to Concord to warn residents.

Glossary

abolitionist (ab-uh-LI-shuhn-ist)—a person who worked to end slavery

account (uh-KOWNT)—an official statement explaining actions or experiences

artisan (AR-tuh-zuhn)—a skilled worker who practices a trade or craft

belfry (BEL-free)—a tower that has one or more bells

colonist (KAH-luh-nist)—a person who lives in a territory that is governed by his or her home country

descendant (di-SEN-duhnt)—a person's child and any family member born after that child

evidence (EV-uh-duhnss)—information, items, and facts that help prove something to be true or false

eyewitness (i-WIT-niss)—a person who has seen or heard something

militiamen (muh-LISH-uh-men)—a group of volunteer citizens who serve as soldiers in emergencies

patriot (PAY-tree-uht)—a person who sided with the colonies before and during the American Revolution

Read More

Doeden, Matt. *The Colonists Revolt: An Interactive American Revolution Adventure*. North Mankato, MN: Capstone Press, 2019.

Katirgis, Jane, and Rose McCarthy. *Meet Paul Revere: Revolutionary Hero*. New York: Enslow Publishing, 2020.

McAneney, Caitie. *Team Time Machine Rides Along with Paul Revere*. New York: Gareth Stevens Publishing, 2020.

Internet Sites

American Revolution
dkfindout.com/us/history/american-revolution/

The Paul Revere House
paulreverehouse.org/

The Revolutionary War Animated Map
battlefields.org/learn/maps/revolutionary-war-animated-map

Index

abolitionists, 15
accounts, 7, 8, 9, 10, 11, 13, 19, 20, 22, 24, 26
American Revolution, 6, 13, 23, 28

Battle of Lexington, 10
belfries, 14, 18
Belknap, Jeremy, 8, 9
Boston, Massachusetts, 4, 5, 14, 18, 19, 20, 23, 28
Boston Massacre of 1770, 7
British soldiers, 4, 5, 6, 7, 10, 11, 19, 23, 24, 26

Charlestown, Massachusetts, 5, 19, 25
Civil War, 14, 15
colonists, 4, 5, 6, 7, 20, 22
Concord, Massachusetts, 4, 5, 6, 12, 19, 23, 26, 27

Dawes, William, 20, 21, 23, 26, 27

Everett, Edward, 12, 13
evidence, 16
eyewitnesses, 7, 13, 22, 26

Gage, Thomas, 24

Holland, Henry Ware, 21
horses, 5, 18, 25, 27

jobs, 7

lanterns, 14, 18, 19, 28
legends, 15, 28
Lexington, Massachusetts, 5, 6, 7, 10, 19, 21, 24, 26, 27
Longfellow, Henry Wadsworth, 14, 15, 16, 18, 20, 21, 22, 24, 26, 28

Massachusetts Historical Society, 8
militiamen, 10, 23
Munro, William, 11, 13

patriots, 5, 6, 7, 11, 12, 18, 20, 23, 25, 26
Phinney, Elias, 10
poetic license, 16
Prescott, Samuel, 26, 27

Warren, Joseph, 20